This Gardening Journal Belongs To:

_____

Monthly
HARVEST CALENDAR

Gardening PROJECTS

YEARLY GOALS

NEW PROJECTS

TECHNIQUES

NOTES

Produce BUDGET

FRUIT/VEGETABLE:	WEIGHT/QTY:	PRICE:	MONTHLY:	YEARLY:

Planting TRACKER

PLANT	QTY	START	TRANSPLANT	SPACING	HARVEST DATE

Garden WISH LIST

What fruits or vegetables would you like to grow?

Garden BUDGET

YEAR: _____

VEGETABLES	AMOUNT:
SUBTOTAL:	

FRUIT	AMOUNT:
SUBTOTAL:	

FLOWERS	AMOUNT:
SUBTOTAL:	

FERTILIZER/MISC	AMOUNT:
SUBTOTAL:	

TOTALS	AMOUNT:
TOTAL:	

SEASON: _____   **YEAR:** _____

CROP	VARIETY	START	TRANSPLANT	BED/ROW

Weekly To Do

WEEK OF: _____

TASK	M	T	W	T	F	S	S	NOTES

ADDITIONAL NOTES

Pest Control

BED/ROW	CROP/FAMILY	PEST	DISEASE	TREATMENT:

Sow

SEASON: _____   **YEAR:** _____

CROP	VARIETY	SOW/TRANSPLANT	BED/ROW

Seed Inventory

YEAR: _____

CROP/VARIETY	SEED COMPANY	PURCHASE DATE	QTY

Seed Purchase

YEAR: _____

CROP/VARIETY	SOURCE	PRICE	QTY

Garden Organizer

BED/ROW	CROPS	SEASON	HARVEST BY	NEXT CROPS

Succession Sowing

YEAR: _____

CROP	SOW DATE	SEASON	BED/ROW	NOTES

Harvest Tracker

YEAR: _____

FRUIT/VEG	WEIGHT/QTY	VARIETY	VALUE	NOTES

Crop Rotation

BED/ROW	CROP	SEASON	NEXT CROP

Growing

YEAR: _____

BED/ROW	NOTES (SOIL TEST, ETC)	NOTES

Planner (Sq. Foot)

YEAR: _____

Seed Packet Info

YEAR: _____

CROP/ VARIETY	SOWING DEPTH	DAYS TO GERMINATE	DAYS TO MATURITY	HARVEST WINDOW

Gardening Expenses

ITEM#	DESCRIPTION	QTY	PRICE	NOTES

TOTAL EXPENSES

Plant List

YEAR:

MOST IMPORTANT CROPS

CROPS TO PRESERVE

Fast Growing Crops

READY IN 30-55 DAYS FOR SUCCESSION SOWING

Gardening To Do List

GARDENING TASKS:

NOTES:

Seasonal To Do List

SPRING

- [ ]
- [ ]
- [ ]
- [ ]
- [ ]
- [ ]
- [ ]
- [ ]

SUMMER

- [ ]
- [ ]
- [ ]
- [ ]
- [ ]
- [ ]
- [ ]
- [ ]

FALL

- [ ]
- [ ]
- [ ]
- [ ]
- [ ]
- [ ]
- [ ]
- [ ]

WINTER

- [ ]
- [ ]
- [ ]
- [ ]
- [ ]
- [ ]
- [ ]
- [ ]

NOTES

Gardening Notes

Monthly
HARVEST CALENDAR

Gardening PROJECTS

YEARLY GOALS

NEW PROJECTS

TECHNIQUES

NOTES

Produce BUDGET

FRUIT/VEGETABLE:	WEIGHT/QTY:	PRICE:	MONTHLY:	YEARLY:

Planting TRACKER

PLANT	QTY	START	TRANSPLANT	SPACING	HARVEST DATE

Garden WISH LIST

What fruits or vegetables would you like to grow?

Garden BUDGET

YEAR: _____

VEGETABLES	AMOUNT:
SUBTOTAL:	

FERTILIZER/MISC	AMOUNT:
SUBTOTAL:	

FRUIT	AMOUNT:
SUBTOTAL:	

FLOWERS	AMOUNT:
SUBTOTAL:	

TOTALS	AMOUNT:
TOTAL:	

Seedlings

SEASON: _____ **YEAR:** _____

CROP	VARIETY	START	TRANSPLANT	BED/ROW

Weekly To Do

WEEK OF: _____

TASK	M	T	W	T	F	S	S	NOTES

ADDITIONAL NOTES

Pest Control

BED/ROW	CROP/FAMILY	PEST	DISEASE	TREATMENT:

Sow

SEASON: _____ **YEAR:** _____

CROP	VARIETY	SOW/TRANSPLANT	BED/ROW

Seed Inventory

YEAR: _____

CROP/VARIETY	SEED COMPANY	PURCHASE DATE	QTY

Seed Purchase

YEAR: _____

CROP/VARIETY	SOURCE	PRICE	QTY

Garden Organizer

BED/ROW	CROPS	SEASON	HARVEST BY	NEXT CROPS

Succession Sowing

YEAR: _____

CROP	SOW DATE	SEASON	BED/ROW	NOTES

Harvest Tracker

YEAR: _____

FRUIT/VEG	WEIGHT/QTY	VARIETY	VALUE	NOTES

Crop Rotation

BED/ROW	CROP	SEASON	NEXT CROP

Growing

YEAR: _____

BED/ROW	NOTES (SOIL TEST, ETC)	NOTES

Planner (Sq. Foot)

Seed Packet Info

YEAR: _____

CROP/ VARIETY	SOWING DEPTH	DAYS TO GERMINATE	DAYS TO MATURITY	HARVEST WINDOW

Gardening Expenses

ITEM#	DESCRIPTION	QTY	PRICE	NOTES

TOTAL EXPENSES

Plant List

YEAR:

MOST IMPORTANT CROPS

CROPS TO PRESERVE

Fast Growing Crops

READY IN 30-55 DAYS FOR SUCCESSION SOWING

Gardening To Do List

GARDENING TASKS:

- [ ]
- [ ]
- [ ]
- [ ]
- [ ]
- [ ]
- [ ]
- [ ]
- [ ]
- [ ]
- [ ]
- [ ]
- [ ]
- [ ]
- [ ]
- [ ]

NOTES:

Seasonal To Do List

SPRING

- [ ]
- [ ]
- [ ]
- [ ]
- [ ]
- [ ]
- [ ]
- [ ]

SUMMER

- [ ]
- [ ]
- [ ]
- [ ]
- [ ]
- [ ]
- [ ]
- [ ]

FALL

- [ ]
- [ ]
- [ ]
- [ ]
- [ ]
- [ ]
- [ ]
- [ ]

WINTER

- [ ]
- [ ]
- [ ]
- [ ]
- [ ]
- [ ]
- [ ]

NOTES

Gardening Notes

Monthly
HARVEST CALENDAR

Gardening PROJECTS

YEARLY GOALS

NEW PROJECTS

TECHNIQUES

NOTES

Produce BUDGET

FRUIT/VEGETABLE:	WEIGHT/QTY:	PRICE:	MONTHLY:	YEARLY:

Planting TRACKER

PLANT	QTY	START	TRANSPLANT	SPACING	HARVEST DATE

Garden WISH LIST

What fruits or vegetables would you like to grow?

Garden BUDGET

YEAR: _____

VEGETABLES	AMOUNT:
SUBTOTAL:	

FERTILIZER/MISC	AMOUNT:
SUBTOTAL:	

FRUIT	AMOUNT:
SUBTOTAL:	

FLOWERS	AMOUNT:
SUBTOTAL:	

TOTALS	AMOUNT:
TOTAL:	

SEASON: _____ **YEAR:** _____

CROP	VARIETY	START	TRANSPLANT	BED/ROW

Weekly To Do

WEEK OF: _____

TASK	M	T	W	T	F	S	S	NOTES

ADDITIONAL NOTES

Pest Control

BED/ROW	CROP/FAMILY	PEST	DISEASE	TREATMENT:

Sow

CROP	VARIETY	SOW/TRANSPLANT	BED/ROW

Seed Inventory

YEAR: _____

CROP/VARIETY	SEED COMPANY	PURCHASE DATE	QTY

Seed Purchase

YEAR: _____

CROP/VARIETY	SOURCE	PRICE	QTY

Garden Organizer

BED/ROW	CROPS	SEASON	HARVEST BY	NEXT CROPS

Succession Sowing

YEAR: _____

CROP	SOW DATE	SEASON	BED/ROW	NOTES

Harvest Tracker

YEAR: _____

FRUIT/VEG	WEIGHT/QTY	VARIETY	VALUE	NOTES

Crop Rotation

YEAR: _____

BED/ROW	CROP	SEASON	NEXT CROP

Growing

YEAR: _____

BED/ROW	NOTES (SOIL TEST, ETC)	NOTES

Planner (Sq. Foot)

Seed Packet Info

YEAR: _____

CROP/ VARIETY	SOWING DEPTH	DAYS TO GERMINATE	DAYS TO MATURITY	HARVEST WINDOW

Gardening Expenses

ITEM#	DESCRIPTION	QTY	PRICE	NOTES

TOTAL EXPENSES

Plant List

YEAR:

MOST IMPORTANT CROPS

CROPS TO PRESERVE

Fast Growing Crops
READY IN 30-55 DAYS FOR SUCCESSION SOWING

Gardening To Do List

GARDENING TASKS:

- [ ]
- [ ]
- [ ]
- [ ]
- [ ]
- [ ]
- [ ]
- [ ]
- [ ]
- [ ]
- [ ]
- [ ]
- [ ]
- [ ]
- [ ]
- [ ]

NOTES:

Seasonal To Do List

SPRING

- [ ]
- [ ]
- [ ]
- [ ]
- [ ]
- [ ]
- [ ]
- [ ]

SUMMER

- [ ]
- [ ]
- [ ]
- [ ]
- [ ]
- [ ]
- [ ]
- [ ]

FALL

- [ ]
- [ ]
- [ ]
- [ ]
- [ ]
- [ ]
- [ ]
- [ ]

WINTER

- [ ]
- [ ]
- [ ]
- [ ]
- [ ]
- [ ]
- [ ]
- [ ]

NOTES

Gardening Notes

Monthly
HARVEST CALENDAR

Gardening PROJECTS

YEARLY GOALS

NEW PROJECTS

TECHNIQUES

NOTES

Produce BUDGET

FRUIT/VEGETABLE:	WEIGHT/QTY:	PRICE:	MONTHLY:	YEARLY:

Planting TRACKER

PLANT	QTY	START	TRANSPLANT	SPACING	HARVEST DATE

Garden WISH LIST

What fruits or vegetables would you like to grow?

Garden BUDGET

YEAR: _____

VEGETABLES	AMOUNT:
SUBTOTAL:	

FRUIT	AMOUNT:
SUBTOTAL:	

FLOWERS	AMOUNT:
SUBTOTAL:	

FERTILIZER/MISC	AMOUNT:
SUBTOTAL:	

TOTALS	AMOUNT:
TOTAL:	

SEASON: .... **YEAR:** ....

CROP	VARIETY	START	TRANSPLANT	BED/ROW

Weekly To Do

WEEK OF: _____

TASK	M	T	W	T	F	S	S	NOTES

ADDITIONAL NOTES

Pest Control

BED/ROW	CROP/FAMILY	PEST	DISEASE	TREATMENT:

Sow

SEASON: _____ **YEAR:** _____

CROP	VARIETY	SOW/TRANSPLANT	BED/ROW

Seed Inventory

YEAR: _____

CROP/VARIETY	SEED COMPANY	PURCHASE DATE	QTY

YEAR: _____

CROP/VARIETY	SOURCE	PRICE	QTY

Garden Organizer

YEAR: _____

BED/ROW	CROPS	SEASON	HARVEST BY	NEXT CROPS

Succession Sowing

YEAR: _____

CROP	SOW DATE	SEASON	BED/ROW	NOTES

Harvest Tracker

YEAR: ....

FRUIT/VEG	WEIGHT/QTY	VARIETY	VALUE	NOTES

Crop Rotation

BED/ROW	CROP	SEASON	NEXT CROP

YEAR: ....

BED/ROW	NOTES (SOIL TEST, ETC)	NOTES

Planner (Sq. Foot)

Seed Packet Info

YEAR: _____

CROP/ VARIETY	SOWING DEPTH	DAYS TO GERMINATE	DAYS TO MATURITY	HARVEST WINDOW

Gardening Expenses

ITEM#	DESCRIPTION	QTY	PRICE	NOTES

TOTAL EXPENSES

Plant List

YEAR:

MOST IMPORTANT CROPS

CROPS TO PRESERVE

Fast Growing Crops
READY IN 30-55 DAYS FOR SUCCESSION SOWING

Gardening To Do List

GARDENING TASKS:

- [ ]
- [ ]
- [ ]
- [ ]
- [ ]
- [ ]
- [ ]
- [ ]
- [ ]
- [ ]
- [ ]
- [ ]
- [ ]
- [ ]
- [ ]
- [ ]

NOTES:

Seasonal To Do List

SPRING

- [ ]
- [ ]
- [ ]
- [ ]
- [ ]
- [ ]
- [ ]
- [ ]

SUMMER

- [ ]
- [ ]
- [ ]
- [ ]
- [ ]
- [ ]
- [ ]
- [ ]

FALL

- [ ]
- [ ]
- [ ]
- [ ]
- [ ]
- [ ]
- [ ]
- [ ]

WINTER

- [ ]
- [ ]
- [ ]
- [ ]
- [ ]
- [ ]
- [ ]

NOTES

Gardening Notes

Monthly
HARVEST CALENDAR

Gardening PROJECTS

YEARLY GOALS

NEW PROJECTS

TECHNIQUES

NOTES

Produce BUDGET

FRUIT/VEGETABLE:	WEIGHT/QTY:	PRICE:	MONTHLY:	YEARLY:

Planting TRACKER

PLANT	QTY	START	TRANSPLANT	SPACING	HARVEST DATE

Garden WISH LIST

What fruits or vegetables would you like to grow?

Garden BUDGET

VEGETABLES	AMOUNT:
SUBTOTAL:	

FERTILIZER/MISC	AMOUNT:
SUBTOTAL:	

FRUIT	AMOUNT:
SUBTOTAL:	

FLOWERS	AMOUNT:
SUBTOTAL:	

TOTALS	AMOUNT:
TOTAL:	

Seedlings

CROP	VARIETY	START	TRANSPLANT	BED/ROW

Weekly To Do

WEEK OF: _____

TASK	M	T	W	T	F	S	S	NOTES

ADDITIONAL NOTES

Pest Control

BED/ROW	CROP/FAMILY	PEST	DISEASE	TREATMENT:

Sow

SEASON: _____ **YEAR:** _____

CROP	VARIETY	SOW/TRANSPLANT	BED/ROW

Seed Inventory

YEAR: _____

CROP/VARIETY	SEED COMPANY	PURCHASE DATE	QTY

Seed Purchase

CROP/VARIETY	SOURCE	PRICE	QTY

Garden Organizer

YEAR: _____

BED/ROW	CROPS	SEASON	HARVEST BY	NEXT CROPS

Succession Sowing

YEAR: _____

CROP	SOW DATE	SEASON	BED/ROW	NOTES

Harvest Tracker

YEAR: _____

FRUIT/VEG	WEIGHT/QTY	VARIETY	VALUE	NOTES

Crop Rotation

YEAR: _____

BED/ROW	CROP	SEASON	NEXT CROP

Growing

YEAR: _____

BED/ROW	NOTES (SOIL TEST, ETC)	NOTES

Planner (Sq. Foot)

YEAR: _____

Seed Packet Info

YEAR: _____

CROP/ VARIETY	SOWING DEPTH	DAYS TO GERMINATE	DAYS TO MATURITY	HARVEST WINDOW

Gardening Expenses

ITEM#	DESCRIPTION	QTY	PRICE	NOTES

TOTAL EXPENSES

Plant List

YEAR:

MOST IMPORTANT CROPS

CROPS TO PRESERVE

Fast Growing Crops
READY IN 30-55 DAYS FOR SUCCESSION SOWING

Gardening To Do List

GARDENING TASKS:

- [ ]
- [ ]
- [ ]
- [ ]
- [ ]
- [ ]
- [ ]
- [ ]
- [ ]
- [ ]
- [ ]
- [ ]
- [ ]
- [ ]
- [ ]
- [ ]
- [ ]

NOTES:

Seasonal To Do List

SPRING

SUMMER

FALL

WINTER

NOTES

Gardening Notes

Monthly
HARVEST CALENDAR

Gardening PROJECTS

YEARLY GOALS

NEW PROJECTS

TECHNIQUES

NOTES

Produce BUDGET

FRUIT/VEGETABLE:	WEIGHT/QTY:	PRICE:	MONTHLY:	YEARLY:

Planting TRACKER

PLANT	QTY	START	TRANSPLANT	SPACING	HARVEST DATE

Garden WISH LIST

What fruits or vegetables would you like to grow?

Garden BUDGET

VEGETABLES	AMOUNT:
SUBTOTAL:	

FRUIT	AMOUNT:
SUBTOTAL:	

FLOWERS	AMOUNT:
SUBTOTAL:	

FERTILIZER/MISC	AMOUNT:
SUBTOTAL:	

TOTALS	AMOUNT:
TOTAL:	

SEASON: _____ **YEAR:** _____

CROP	VARIETY	START	TRANSPLANT	BED/ROW

Weekly To Do

WEEK OF: _____

TASK	M	T	W	T	F	S	S	NOTES

ADDITIONAL NOTES

Pest Control

BED/ROW	CROP/FAMILY	PEST	DISEASE	TREATMENT:

Sow

CROP	VARIETY	SOW/TRANSPLANT	BED/ROW

Seed Inventory

YEAR: _____

CROP/VARIETY	SEED COMPANY	PURCHASE DATE	QTY

Seed Purchase

YEAR: _____

CROP/VARIETY	SOURCE	PRICE	QTY

Garden Organizer

YEAR:

BED/ROW	CROPS	SEASON	HARVEST BY	NEXT CROPS

Succession Sowing

YEAR: _____

CROP	SOW DATE	SEASON	BED/ROW	NOTES

Harvest Tracker

YEAR: _____

FRUIT/VEG	WEIGHT/QTY	VARIETY	VALUE	NOTES

Crop Rotation

YEAR: _____

BED/ROW	CROP	SEASON	NEXT CROP

Growing

YEAR: _____

BED/ROW	NOTES (SOIL TEST, ETC)	NOTES

Planner (Sq. Foot)

YEAR: _____

Seed Packet Info

YEAR: _____

CROP/ VARIETY	SOWING DEPTH	DAYS TO GERMINATE	DAYS TO MATURITY	HARVEST WINDOW

Gardening Expenses

ITEM#	DESCRIPTION	QTY	PRICE	NOTES

TOTAL EXPENSES

Plant List

YEAR:

MOST IMPORTANT CROPS

CROPS TO PRESERVE

Fast Growing Crops
READY IN 30-55 DAYS FOR SUCCESSION SOWING

Gardening To Do List

GARDENING TASKS:

NOTES:

Seasonal To Do List

SPRING

- [ ]
- [ ]
- [ ]
- [ ]
- [ ]
- [ ]
- [ ]
- [ ]

SUMMER

- [ ]
- [ ]
- [ ]
- [ ]
- [ ]
- [ ]
- [ ]
- [ ]

FALL

- [ ]
- [ ]
- [ ]
- [ ]
- [ ]
- [ ]
- [ ]
- [ ]

WINTER

- [ ]
- [ ]
- [ ]
- [ ]
- [ ]
- [ ]
- [ ]
- [ ]

NOTES

Gardening Notes

Gardening Notes

Gardening Notes

_____

_____

_____

_____

_____

_____

_____

_____

_____

_____

_____

Gardening Notes

Gardening Notes

Printed in Great Britain
by Amazon

11072631R00086